MW01627195

Horses, My Beginnings
An Inspiring Chapter Book for Girls to Boost Confidence, Develop Inner Strength, and Growth Mindset

Written by Sophia Anna Ritter
Illustrations by Cameron Coetzer
Production management by Magdalene Ward

For information address LittleBigPage, 312 W. 2nd St #1934
Casper, WY 82601, United States.

Paperback ISBN: 9788367973373

First Edition

HORSES, MY BEGINNINGS

SOPHIA A. RITTER

You can **download the free audiobook** version of this book.

Go to the *last page* for more information!

Contents

Jingle Jangle
Susan
Lucy
Avril

Mr. Blaze
Dad
Mom
Nancy

Introduction

Moving to a new town can be challenging for any girl. With all her old friends living miles away, Avril decides it's easier to lose herself in books than try to make new friends. Avril's parents encourage her to get out more often and try new activities. However, nothing they suggest interests her.

But when Avril finds out a nearby riding school is offering riding lessons for kids, everything changes. Suddenly, going to riding school becomes the main focus of her life. Through her experiences at riding school, Avril not only learns how to ride horses and make new friends—she also learns important life skills such as patience and how to learn from mistakes, manage anxiety, let go of perfectionism, ask for help when needed, and embrace the good that can come from unexpected changes.

As you follow Avril on her riding school adventures, you'll discover some valuable tips on how to deal with challenging issues in your life. You'll see that even the most difficult problems can be overcome with courage, persistence, and help from your friends, teachers, and family.

CHAPTER ONE

Try Somthing New

AS THE SEPTEMBER sun's early morning rays peeked through the window, Avril nestled in the cozy living room chair, preparing to embark on an exciting literary adventure. But just as she opened her book, Avril heard her parents coming down the stairs.

"Avril, are you up already?" her mother asked.

"Yes, Mom. I'm up," Avril replied, groaning softly to herself.

Avril was eleven years old and in the sixth grade. She loved to get up early so she could read before anyone else was awake. This was her private time. A time when no one was talking, playing the radio, or turning the television up so loud that she could hardly focus on her story. And more importantly, no one was asking her questions.

"Do you have anything fun planned for the day?" her father asked.

"Yes," Avril said. "I plan to read the book I borrowed from the library. It's about a girl who finds a unicorn in the woods. They go on an exciting adventure to save the people of the town from an evil monster."

Avril hoped the answer would satisfy her parents.

"Reading is wonderful," her mother said, "but the radio announcer said this will be a beautiful sunny day. Have you thought about going over to the playground? I saw some girls about your age playing soccer there last Saturday. I'm sure they would be happy for you to join them."

"Soccer?" Avril said. "I don't know anything about playing soccer."

"Wouldn't it be fun to learn?" her mother asked. "If you'd like, we could get you signed up for the local youth soccer program. I saw a poster about it at the grocery store last week."

"I don't want to kick a ball around in the park. I want to read!"

"Avril," her father replied, "I'm glad you love to read, but we're worried that you spend far too much time at home with your nose in a book. You need to get out in the world, do things kids enjoy, and make new friends."

Avril glanced down at her book, but she knew that trying to get back into the story was useless. Her parents' intrusion had broken the spell.

"I know things haven't been easy for you since we moved," Avril's mother said, "but you won't make new friends sitting at home. Have you made any friends at school yet?"

"I have all the friends I need in my books," Avril snapped. "They are here waiting for me whenever I want them. Not only that, but I can travel to all sorts of places just by reading! I can explore the pyramids of Egypt, watch exotic animals in the Amazon jungle—I can even board a spaceship and go anywhere in the universe!"

Avril's parents looked at each other for a moment. Then her mother said, "Avril, your father and I have come up with a list of activities we think you might like."

"You have?" Avril asked suspiciously.

"We'd like for you to look it over and pick four or

five activities. Then, in the next few weeks try them a few times. If you agree to do that, you can read all you want. Deal?"

Avril nodded, reluctantly agreeing to her parents' plan. She picked five activities from the list and put the list on the kitchen table. Her choices were piano lessons, tennis lessons, dance lessons, a painting class, and a bird-watching group for kids that met in a nearby park.

Then Avril headed to her room with her unicorn book.

As she sat on the edge of her bed, Avril wondered what the kids at these new activities would be like. She still missed her friends from her old school. Sometimes they talked on the phone. A few times, they had even visited, but it just wasn't the same as when they attended school together.

Avril had tried to make friends at her new school, but she didn't seem to fit in with any of the friend groups. She always had to start conversations, and none of the other students ever had much to say to her. The conversations never seemed to last very long. It was much easier to get lost in a book than try to navigate the social scene at school.

"I wish Dad's company hadn't made us move," Avril sighed.

While Avril was bemoaning her fate, her parents were busy putting together a schedule based on the activities she had picked from the list.

Avril kept her promise.

She tried at least a few new activities every week. She did her best to enjoy each activity, but none of them sparked her interest.

"How do you like piano?" her mother asked one morning.

"It's all right, but not much fun," Avril replied.

"How about painting?" her father asked. "I always loved to paint when I was your age."

"It's ok," Avril answered, "but every time I think I might like painting, the teacher tells me I'm doing something wrong."

"Like what?" her father asked.

"The teacher tells me that I need to rinse my paintbrush more before I switch colors. By the time I rinse my brush enough to make her happy, I forget what I was going to paint."

"How about bird watching?" her mother asked. "Did you like that, and did you make any new friends?"

"Not really," Avril replied. "The other kids know lots more about birds than I do. By the time I figure out what bird it might be, some other kid has already identified it."

"Did you like anything you tried?" her mother asked.

Avril shook her head. "No, not really."

"Alright, Avril," her father said with a sigh. "We haven't hit on the right thing yet, but at least you're trying."

"How would you like to go to a movie this afternoon?" her mother asked brightly. "I hear the theater downtown is showing a movie about a girl who lives on a horse ranch. We thought that might be a good reward for trying new things."

"Really?" Avril squeaked. "That does sound like fun!"

To Avril, a good movie was almost as exciting as reading, and if there wasn't a movie at the theater about unicorns, horses would be the next best thing. Avril could hardly wait until it was time to go to the theater.

Once they arrived, she loved every minute of the movie. As she watched, Avril imagined how much fun it would be to ride a horse, feeling the joy and freedom of the wind blowing through her hair.

As the movie ended, Avril told her parents, "That was the best movie ever! I wish I had a horse to ride." Her mother and father smiled, happy that she had enjoyed the show.

On the way out of the theater, Avril saw a poster that stopped her in her tracks. "Look!" she exclaimed. "Someone is advertising horseback riding lessons for kids. Forget all those other activities—this is what I want to do!"

"Horseback riding lessons?" her mother asked. "Isn't that dangerous? You might fall off and get hurt."

"I don't think that's a good idea," her father said. "Your mother's right—you might get hurt. Horses are huge animals. They can jump and kick without warning. Maybe we can discuss it again when you're a little older."

"You wanted me to get interested in something besides books," Avril said, "and when I do, you tell me I'm not allowed to do it!" She could not stop the tears that flowed from her eyes.

For the rest of the afternoon, Avril was sullen. As soon as she got home, she went to her room and lost herself in her books.

When her mother called her to supper, Avril came downstairs and ate without saying a word.

"Are you alright?" her father asked. "I've never seen you so quiet at mealtime."

Avril looked down at her plate for a minute and then said, "I'm sorry about my outburst. But when I saw the poster about horseback riding lessons, I knew that's exactly what I wanted to do. Why can't I at least try it?"

Avril's father sighed and looked over at her mother.

Finally, her mother said, "Ok, we'll go out and look at the riding school, but no promises. We want to make sure it's safe before we let you enroll."

Avril was over the moon with joy. She could hardly wait until the next week when her parents would take her to the riding school. In her mind, she was already riding. Nothing would stop her dream of horseback riding now!

CHAPTER TWO

Visiting the Riding School

WHEN THEY arrived at the riding school, Avril could hardly contain her excitement.

The scent of freshly mowed hay greeted her as soon as she opened the car door. At least a dozen horses were grazing in the field. Avril wondered which one she would get to ride.

The riding teacher, a smiling lady with long braids and a cowboy hat met Avril and her parents. "Hello, my name is Susan," she said. "Welcome to my horse farm!"

"Nice to meet you," Avril said. "My name is Avril, and these are my parents. I saw your poster at the movie theater, and I'd love to learn how to ride horses!"

"How long have you been teaching horseback riding lessons?" Avril's mother asked.

"I bought the horse farm five years ago," Susan said, "and I've been teaching horseback riding lessons for three years. I have a nice group of horses for our students to work with. Some of our horses are very gentle—just perfect for children who are riding for the first time."

Susan assured Avril's parents that every possible precaution was used to keep the children safe, and Avril's parents agreed to let her sign up for riding lessons.

"Thank you," Susan said, smiling. "It's great that Avril is so interested in horses, and I know she will enjoy the riding lessons. Some of the students here are just about her age."

Susan then invited Avril to go to the stable and meet the horse she would be riding.

"This is Jingle Jangle," Susan said brightly as she pointed to the light tan (buckskin) horse. "She is a gentle horse that loves children. I know you want to ride her, but first, you must let her get to know you."

Avril nodded, feeling her excitement build.

"First," Susan said, "you should stand slightly to the side of the horse and slowly reach your hand towards her. Then, let her smell the back of your hand. And while you're reaching your hand out, you should talk softly to her."

Avril carefully followed Susan's instructions. "Oh, you wonderful, beautiful horse," Avril said as she held her hand near Jingle Jangle's face. The horse softly whinnied in response.

Avril could barely contain her joy as she and Jingle Jangle got to know each other. Once they were acquainted, Susan showed Avril how to brush, groom, and saddle her.

* * *

Finally, it was time for Avril to sit in the saddle, ready for her first riding lesson!

Susan led Jingle Jangle out into the riding path. Avril held onto the reins and did her best to balance. Even with Jingle Jangle walking slowly, balancing on a horse was more difficult than Avril expected. But gradually, she got the hang of it. Her parents stood by the stable and watched.

As they were walking on the path that led around the pasture, with Susan leading Jingle Jangle, Avril noticed that Lucy, one of the girls from her middle school was there too.

"Hey, Lucy," Avril yelled, "I didn't know you rode horses!"

Lucy turned around and waved.

The sudden yelling spooked Jingle Jangle. She broke away from Susan, picked up her pace, and started galloping across the field. Avril tried her best to balance, but the horse's sudden motions made staying in the saddle nearly impossible.

"Susan!" Avril yelled across the field in a panic. "What do I do?"

Susan ran to catch up with Jingle Jangle, saying, "Whoa, steady, careful!" to the horse. But it was too late.

Avril slid off the horse's back and landed in a mud puddle.

Avril's parents screamed in terror. Lucy turned her horse around and rode back to the scene of the accident.

"Are you alright?" Susan said breathlessly as she ran over to Avril.

"I'm fine," Avril replied, feeling scared and embarrassed. She stood up slowly and tried to wipe the mud off her clothes.

"That's it!" Avril's mother said, checking her daughter all over for any injuries. "No more riding school for you!"

"No more riding lessons," her father declared, looking at the horse with terror. "Let's go home before you have another accident!"

As Avril walked to the car, she looked back longingly at the horses in the pasture.

She couldn't hold back her tears as they drove home. Her dream was so close to happening but had been ripped away by a silly mistake.

That evening, Avril decided to talk to Lucy, the girl from school who she saw riding at Susan's farm. Even if she never got to take riding lessons again, at least she knew that they had a common interest. Avril looked up Lucy's number on the list from school and gave her a call.

"Hi, Lucy," she said. "This is Avril. It was nice seeing you at the riding school today. I didn't know you liked horses. My family is new in town, and it's been really tough finding friends who like the same things I do."

"I know," Lucy said. "It's hard to talk horses when nearly everyone else wants to talk about video games and superheroes."

Avril smiled. Finally, she found someone in her class who she might be able to bond with!

"Sorry you had an accident on your first ride," Lucy said, "but I'm glad you didn't get hurt."

"So am I," Avril replied. "I sure hope my parents change their mind and let me take riding lessons."

"Hopefully they will—once they calm down," Lucy said encouragingly.

"You're a really good rider! I bet you never fell off a horse."

"I almost did," Lucy confessed. "When I started riding, I wasn't very good at keeping my balance in the saddle."

"Really? But you ride so well! You make riding look easy."

"There's a lot more to horseback riding than most people think, but Susan is a great teacher. If your parents let you take lessons again, I know she'll give you lots of great tips."

The following morning, Avril brought up the subject at the breakfast table.

“I understand what I did wrong,” she told her parents. “I shouldn’t have yelled across the field—especially when Jingle Jangle and I were just getting to know each other. If you let me take riding lessons again, I promise I will follow my riding teacher’s instructions to the letter!”

“You already fell off once,” her mother said. “It’s too risky.”

“But learning to ride a horse is the most important thing in the world to me!” Avril insisted.

After much debate, her parents realized that Avril wasn’t going to give up until she was taking lessons at the riding school again.

“All right, you win,” her father said reluctantly. “You can start taking riding lessons again next week. But please do be careful!”

Chapter Three

Avril's Second Chance

Avril could barely contain her excitement about going back to riding school. She could hardly wait until she was back at Susan's farm, riding Jingle Jangle again.

No matter how hard she tried to stay focused at school, thoughts of Jingle Jangle kept popping up. At last, the final bell rang, and school was over for the day. Avril gathered her books and rushed to Lucy's locker so they could talk about horses and riding.

"Hi, Avril!" Lucy said. "Are your parents going to let you return to riding school?"

"They are!" Avril replied, beaming with excitement. "But I'll have to be extra careful. If I have another fall, I doubt they'll let me go back."

"Great! I've had so much fun since I learned how to ride. My horse and I have gone on all sorts of adventures.

Just last week, I rode on a path in the forest just outside of town. I saw some blackberries and stopped to gather them. Just as I was putting on my backpack to head back on the trail, I saw a beautiful deer and her fawn by the stream. Another time, I rode out along the path by the river and stopped to watch a magnificent eagle gliding through the sky."

"Wow, I can hardly wait until I can ride well enough to go off Susan's farm and do things like that!" Avril laughed. "But first, I have to learn how to balance in the saddle and not spook my horse!"

The girls gathered the books they needed for homework and said goodbye.

Before leaving school, Avril made a quick stop at the school library and checked out a book about horses and horseback riding.

"Did you have a good day at school?" Avril's mother asked as she hopped into the car.

"I sure did!" Avril answered. "Lucy, the girl at Susan's farm, told me all about her riding adventures, and I checked out a book about riding. I can hardly wait to read it!"

"Remember you have homework," her mother said. "You also promised Miss Johnson that you would feed her cats while she's away."

"I know," Avril answered. "I haven't forgotten."

Avril ran up to her room. She plopped into her chair and opened the book. As she read and looked at the pictures, she filled her notebook with drawings of horses and how they looked when they ran, walked, and soared over jumps. She also went on YouTube to watch videos of horses and riders performing these skills.

One chapter immediately caught Avril's eye. It described a fun riding skill that she had never heard of. It was called dressage, and it almost looked like the horse in the picture was dancing! Avril decided that the next time she was at riding school, she had to try it.

* * *

"Hello! Glad you came back," Susan said as Avril jumped out of her parents' car. "Sometimes it can be hard to get back into riding after you've had a fall."

"I am more than ready," Avril announced. "I can hardly wait to get back in the saddle!"

"That's a great attitude to have," Susan said as she walked Avril to the stable. "Here's an apple you can give Jingle Jangle before you ride her today. She loves apples."

Jingle Jangle greeted Avril with a soft neigh and a shake of her head. Remembering what Susan had taught her, Avril held her hand out and talked softly to the horse. Avril handed Jingle Jangle the apple, and she happily ate it. Then Avril brushed Jingle Jangle and gently stroked her head.

Once they had spent some time bonding, Susan asked, "Are you ready?" Avril nodded, and Susan helped her onto Jingle Jangle's saddle.

"Let's take it a little slower today," Susan cautioned. "It takes time to learn how to balance on a horse. I know you don't want to have another fall."

They walked the path around the field once, then stopped in front of the stable.

"Good job!" Susan said. "You followed my instructions, and your horse stayed calm."

"Thanks!" Avril beamed. "I want to show you something."

"What?" Susan asked with a puzzled look on her face.

Avril picked up Jingle Jangle's reins and tried to copy what the rider had done in the book. Instead of happily prancing like the horse Avril read about, Jingle Jangle looked confused. She stood in place, looked towards Susan, and whinnied softly.

"I know what you are trying to do," Susan said gently, "but Jingle Jangle doesn't. She has never been taught dressage riding."

"She hasn't?" Avril asked with a puzzled look on her face.

"No," Susan said. "Jingle Jangle is a very gentle horse that we use for beginners. This is only your second riding lesson. When you have more experience, you can try that skill with one of our more spirited horses."

Avril looked down at the ground, feeling embarrassed.

"Let's try another walk around the path," Susan suggested.

Avril perked up and went back to focusing on the task of balancing on Jingle Jangle's saddle. She continued working on her balancing skills until her riding lesson was over and it was time to go home.

"How did things go today?" her mother asked.

"Great!" Avril said. "Susan helped me learn how to balance better so I don't fall off again."

"I'm glad," her mother said, letting out a sigh of relief.

* * *

When it was time for her next riding lesson. Avril couldn't stop thinking about a TV show she had watched the night before. It was a western, and the cowboys' horses in the show ran as fast as lightning!

Avril and Jingle Jangle took a few minutes to visit. Then Susan helped Avril up onto the saddle.

"Do you think you're ready to ride her around the field by yourself?" Susan asked.

"I sure do!" Avril replied.

"Okay, but remember, you're still new to riding. You need to take it slowly."

"I will!" Avril promised as she headed out of the stable and onto the riding path.

At first, Avril did take it slow. She made sure not to prompt Jingle Jangle to walk any faster than she could balance.

On the second trip around the field, Avril started thinking about the horses she saw on TV the night before. She imagined what it would feel like to be on a fast horse, riding like the wind.

Avril heard Susan saying something in the distance, but she was too far into her daydream to pay attention. As Avril slipped even deeper into her daydream, Jingle Jangle felt Avril nudging her forward and picked up her speed.

"You need to slow her down!" Susan said. "Sit tall and relax your legs."

Avril snapped out of her daydream. She realized that Jingle Jangle was trotting faster than she was used to. Because of this, she was having trouble matching her movements with the horse's. Avril's balance was so bad that she almost fell off!

Susan ran over to Jingle Jangle and held her bridle. Avril took a few deep breaths.

"Avril, you need to stay focused and stick to the basics," Susan said. "You are still a new rider. You can't jump into the deep end without knowing how to swim first."

"Sorry," Avril answered, feeling shocked at how quickly the situation had gotten out of control.

For the rest of the riding lesson, Avril kept her mind off the TV show horses—she was not ready to ride like those cowboys quite yet!

But she was still determined to try new things.

In every riding lesson that month, Avril tried to do at least one thing she had read about in the book about horse riding. Some days, with Susan's help, Avril was able to get Jingle Jangle to try something a little different. That gave Avril hope that she was becoming a better rider.

Jingle Jangle often struggled to understand what Avril wanted, though. One day, she became so confused that she turned around and walked back into the stable halfway through the riding lesson.

Avril's face was red with embarrassment as she got off Jingle Jangle. She felt like she was making no progress at all! At the same time, the other students at the riding school were becoming better riders in every lesson.

And then it hit her.

Susan had been right all along. Even the books and the trainer in the videos she watched on YouTube said new riders must learn the basics of riding before they try to master fancy skills.

Trying to rush things hadn't helped Avril's progress one bit. It had only led to disappointment and frustration. Avril knew the answer was to slow down and learn to be patient with herself.

The next day at breakfast, Avril's father put down his newspaper and asked, "How are your riding lessons coming? Are they as much fun as you thought they'd be?"

Avril took a deep breath and said, "Riding horses is harder than I thought."

"Do you want to try something else instead?" her mother offered.

"No!" Avril answered. "I still want to learn all about horses and how to ride them. I want that more than anything."

"Is there a problem with your riding lessons?" her father asked.

"Not anymore. I have finally figured out what I've been doing wrong. I wanted to try all the things I read about in that book, but I'm not ready for that just yet.

From now on, I will focus on the basics, just like Susan told me to. I want to learn how to take care of a horse and do barn chores and grooming. I want to learn everything Susan can teach me about being a good rider."

"Sounds like a plan!" her father said.

Avril still read books about horseback riding, but she no longer thought she had to try everything she read about. Instead, she talked to Susan about what she read. Susan promised Avril that she would slowly add new riding skills to her lessons as soon as she was ready.

When Avril was no longer pushing herself to try new riding skills, she started to build a stronger bond with Jingle Jangle than she ever had before. This made riding her feel more natural and fun.

"I'm very proud of you," Susan said. "Now that you've taken time to learn the basics, your riding skills are becoming so much better!"

Avril smiled and said, "Thanks for being patient with me and my impatience."

Chapter Four

No More Mistakes!

The beautiful early autumn afternoon was sunny and warm. All the students were assembled at Susan's riding school, waiting for their lessons to start. Susan walked out of the stable and greeted them with a big smile.

"I have a special treat for you today," she said.

"What is it?" Avril asked, jumping down off the wooden fence.

"Nancy, a friend of mine is in the area for a riding competition," Susan said. "She is going to show you what a skilled rider with years of practice can do!"

Avril climbed back up onto the wooden fence to get a good view of the field, and the other riding students all joined her.

Moments later, Nancy and her horse galloped into the field. Avril and the other riding students could hardly contain their excitement.

The horse was galloping like the wind! Yet Nancy had no trouble staying on its back. They circled the field, galloping even faster. On the next pass, the horse effortlessly jumped over some hurdles.

Nancy gave the horse directions to slow down and do a lovely trot. These were skills from the books Avril loved to read. Avril turned to Lucy and said, "I've made a decision."

"What is it?" Lucy asked, her eyes widening.

"I'm going to be as good as that rider, if not better!"

"That's a really big goal," Lucy cautioned.

"Yes, it is," Avril said, standing up to her full height, "and I know exactly how to make it happen."

"Lots of practice?"

"That's the plan. From now on, I will do my best not to make any mistakes. If I don't make mistakes, everything I do will be better and better!"

When Avril got home, she took out a big sheet of paper. She made a sign that read, "I don't make mistakes!" She also made signs that said "Mistakes are bad!" and "Everything I do will be perfect!"

Avril took some tape and put the signs up all around her room.

She went to sleep telling herself, "I don't make mistakes...I don't make mistakes...I don't make mistakes."

When she woke up the next morning, Avril double-checked her homework. She wanted to make one hundred percent sure that all the answers were right.

Then she read her schedule for the day. She had school, then riding lessons in the late afternoon.

"Everything I do today will be perfect!" she told herself.

At school, Avril listened carefully to everything her teachers said. She took more notes than usual.

When school was over, Avril's mother picked her up and drove her to Susan's farm. As they arrived, Avril saw that Susan had put up a few scarecrows by the entrance. In the distance, she could see some children picking berries outside the riding field.

"I won't make any mistakes today," she told herself. "My riding lesson will be perfect!"

But as they walked up to the stable, Avril realized she had left her notebook at school. Without her notes, she wouldn't be able to do her homework that evening.

"Noooooo!" Avril yelled. "This can't be happening."

"What's wrong?" her mother asked. Avril told her, and they both hurried back to the car. They returned to the school, but by the time they got there, the janitor was locking the doors for the day. Thankfully, he was kind enough to open the door back up and let them in.

"I promised myself that I wouldn't make mistakes," Avril moaned.

With her notebook now safely in her backpack, Avril jumped back into the car, and her mother continued to drive her to Susan's farm.

By the time she arrived, all the other students were already there. "I thought you forgot to come," Lucy said. "You always get here before the rest of us."

"I had to go back to school and get my notebook," Avril said. "I was in such a hurry to get here that I forgot it."

Just then, Susan came out to greet the students. She took them to the stable to mount their horses.

Still out of breath, Avril threw her leg over Jingle Jangle and took the reins.

For the entire riding lesson, Avril tried her best to do exactly what Susan told her. She did not try to do anything from the videos.

Susan was happy to see Avril had kept her promise to focus on the basics of riding.

Once they returned to the stables, Avril told Susan, "Thank you for letting us watch your friend ride. One of these days, I will be just as good as she is!"

"I bet you will be," Susan said. "But remember, it takes practice and patience."

When Avril got home, her mother was waiting by the door.

"I got a call from your teacher," her mother said. "Mrs. Dutton told me that you accidentally turned in your riding schedule with your math homework. She wanted to let you know so you wouldn't worry about it."

“Thanks, Mom,” Avril said as she headed upstairs toward her room.

Avril could hardly believe it. No matter how hard she tried, she was still making mistakes!

The next day, things didn’t go any better.

Avril got two answers wrong on her math test. She almost tripped over her shoelaces in gym class. In her rush to get to the school bus, she forgot to zip her book bag and her books fell out everywhere.

All these mistakes made Avril wonder if she had set an impossible goal.

Avril said to herself, “Maybe I should write down all my mistakes. Then I’ll make sure not to make them again.”

Avril got her notebook and wrote down every mistake she made. Not just mistakes in her riding lessons but also mistakes she made at home and school. She looked at the list before she went to bed. Then she read it again in the morning before breakfast.

The list got longer and longer. It seemed the harder Avril tried to avoid mistakes, the more she made.

When Avril went to her next riding lesson, Susan and Nancy were talking. Susan said, "Avril, you are getting very good at the basics. Would you like to try something new?"

Avril said, "Not today. I already made three mistakes since breakfast, and I don't want to make any more!"

"All right, we can wait until your next lesson," Susan said as she helped Avril onto her horse.

Jingle Jangle could tell that Avril was nervous. Her back and arms were stiff, which made her riding rigid.

When she signaled for Jingle Jangle to turn, she pulled her reins in the wrong direction. If Jingle Jangle had followed Avril's instructions, she would have walked right into the fence!

Jingle Jangle didn't know what Avril wanted her to do. She walked slowly into the field behind the barn. She stood there until Susan came and led her back into the stable.

Avril hopped off Jingle Jangle and sat down on a haystack. She buried her face in her hands and started to cry.

Nancy, who was helping Susan at the farm, saw Avril crying and walked over to comfort her. "Susan tells me you don't want to make any mistakes," she said.

"I tried my best not to make mistakes," Avril said, sobbing, "but I keep making them anyway!"

"Everyone makes mistakes."

"Even you?" Avril asked, looking up.

"Of course! When I first started riding, I made so many mistakes I thought I'd never get the hang of it."

Avril looked at her in surprise. "But you're perfect!"

Nancy laughed and shook her head. "Far from it! When I first started riding, I fell off the horse. I forgot to tie the reins. I even spooked my horse a few times, but each time, I learned something. That's how I got to be the rider I am now."

Avril thought about what Nancy said. She also thought about her list of mistakes and how much pressure she had put on herself.

When Avril got home, she picked up her notebook. She tore out the list of mistakes. Then she wadded it up and threw it in the trash.

Then Avril started two new lists. A list of things she wanted to learn and a list of things she was grateful for.

"I'm going to try my best," Avril said to herself, as a sense of warmth spread through her chest. "I know I will make mistakes, but that's okay. Every mistake is just a chance to learn."

At her next riding lesson, Avril climbed happily onto Jingle Jangle's back. She was ready to learn how to be a champion rider, no matter how many mistakes it took to do it!

Chapter Five

The Horse Show

Avril had been riding Jingle Jangle for several months now. Her skill and confidence grew with each lesson.

One morning at breakfast, Avril's father said, "It sounds like you're pretty excited about the horse show that's coming up in a few months. I heard you talking to Lucy about it."

"I sure am!" Avril replied. "After all these months of riding Jingle Jangle, I have a really great bond with her. I always spend time talking to her before each ride. When I give her directions to go faster, slow down, or jump, she does exactly what I ask her to do. We make a great team, and I know we can win!"

"Susan tells me that you're getting to be quite a rider," Avril's mother said.

Avril beamed as she finished eating her cereal.

"But remember, lots of riding students will be competing," her mother cautioned, "and not everyone can win."

"I know," Avril sighed. She never liked it when her parents used their "don't get your hopes up too high" voices. They were her hopes, and Avril felt it was her right to get them just as high as she wanted!

"I do have one thing going for me," Avril said. "No one in my class seems to be more focused on their training than I am."

"How about your friend Lucy?" her mother asked. "Will she be competing against you?"

"No, Lucy is a second-year riding student, so she will be competing in a different division."

Later that day, Avril and the other students met at the riding school. They were all excited about riding in the competition.

Susan greeted Avril and said, "I think you are ready for a more energetic horse. I want you to try riding Mr. Blaze today."

When Avril heard this, she could hardly contain her excitement. Riding fast, energetic horses had been her dream since her parents took her to see the horse movie.

Then, she started to panic.

"It's too close to the competition to change horses!" Avril blurted out. "Jingle Jangle and I have a great bond. We get along great, and I know exactly how she is going to react."

"That is true," Susan said, "but the riding competition is a few months away. I thought you might enjoy a new challenge. It's up to you, but riding a beginner's horse like Jingle Jangle won't win you a prize."

"You've always wanted to ride a faster horse," Lucy said. "Now here's your opportunity!"

Susan could see that Avril was unsure of what to do. "Come over to the stable and meet Mr. Blaze," she encouraged. "He is a fine horse, and I think you'll enjoy getting to know him."

They walked to the stable. Mr. Blaze was standing by the stall door, waiting to be ridden. He was a chestnut brown horse with a white star marking on his forehead. When Susan and Avril approached, Mr. Blaze nickered happily to greet them.

"Would you like to try bonding with him and riding him a few times before you decide?" Susan offered.

Avril looked up at Mr. Blaze. She could see from the look in his eyes that he was full of energy. She knew that riding him would be a challenge, but she had to try.

Avril said, "Hello, Mr. Blaze."

He looked down at her and neighed.

Avril slowly reached her hand out to Mr Blaze and quietly talked to him so he could get to know her.

"Are you ready?" Susan asked.

Avril nodded, and Susan helped her onto Mr. Blaze's saddle.

Within moments, Avril found out that Mr. Blaze was a very fast runner. It was all she could do to stay on his back. When she prompted him to jump, he leaped higher than Jingle Jangle ever had when they jumped over the low poles that Susan had set up on the ground.

Avril started to wonder if she was ready for this new challenge.

Every time Avril came to riding lessons, she felt more anxious. She was worried that Mr. Blaze would be even

more energetic than the time before. It was hard not to let her anxiety get the best of her. Even worse, Avril knew that her anxiety was making Mr. Blaze anxious too.

Because of this, Avril did her best to calm her anxiety before she went to the stable. On the days when she was able to stay calm, she and Mr. Blaze worked well together. When she was nervous, so was her horse.

One day, a trainer who was a judge at the upcoming competition came to the riding school to talk to the students. He told them what it would be like to compete and the skills they would be required to demonstrate. Then he asked the students if they had any questions.

Avril raised her hand. "I am registered to ride Mr. Blaze, but would it be possible for me to ride a different horse in the show?"

The trainer nodded. "As a first-year rider, you are allowed to. However, in advanced competitions, you will not have the luxury of doing so."

His words echoed in Avril's mind for the rest of the day. She wanted to be a skilled rider who could ride any horse, but the idea of riding Mr. Blaze in a competition filled her with anxiety. The very idea of it made her stomach churn.

That evening, Avril thought about how well she rode Mr. Blaze when she was able to stay calm. Then she decided what she would do.

At her next riding lesson, Avril told Susan, "I've made up my mind. I'm going to ride Mr. Blaze in the competition."

Susan smiled and said, "I'm proud of you!"

Then she helped Avril as she continued to go over basic riding skills with Mr. Blaze. Avril was making every effort to bond with the horse, but each time she rode him, his fast pace and high jumps kept her on edge.

As the competition neared, Avril's anxiety grew worse. Mr. Blaze seemed to pick up on her every fear. This made his own behavior jerky and unpredictable.

"What am I doing wrong?" Avril wailed to Susan after a stressful ride.

"You have the riding skills," Susan said. "You just need to work on staying relaxed."

* * *

It was the day of the competition. Avril's anxiety was worse than ever! No matter how hard she tried, she couldn't make herself go near Mr. Blaze.

Avril locked herself in the bathroom at the stable and hoped no one would find her.

When Susan noticed Avril was missing, she looked everywhere. Susan called Avril until she finally answered, but she refused to come out of the bathroom.

"Avril, you're a good rider," Susan said. "I know you can do this. Think of all the hours you practiced."

But Avril was so anxious that she couldn't unlock the door.

Avril's parents arrived to watch the competition. Susan told them what was happening, and they came over to the bathroom.

"Avril, showing horses is your dream," her father said. "Everyone is anxious the first time. Please...come out."

Then her mother said, "Avril, everyone wants to watch you ride. We know you can do it!"

When Nancy heard that Avril had locked herself in the bathroom, she also tried to help. "Avril, I understand exactly how you feel. I was very nervous at my first riding competition too, but once I got out on the field with my horse, all the nerves just seemed to melt away."

Avril took a deep breath and unlocked the door. As she left the bathroom, Avril heard the horses neighing in the distance and wondered if one of them was Mr. Blaze. She remembered how much she wanted to enter and win this event. Slowly, she felt her courage start to return.

Avril found Mr. Blaze waiting for her in the stable. She approached him and said, "I'm sorry for being so anxious. You're a great horse, and I know we can win this together."

Avril whispered soothing words to Mr. Blaze and gently stroked his face. Soon, she felt her anxiety melting away.

Avril mounted Mr. Blaze and rode to the area where the competitors were waiting for their turn. Riding teachers, parents, students, and other horse lovers from the community were seated in the bleachers, watching the event.

Mr. Blaze performed beautifully in the competition. She rode him with total confidence. He followed her every command to walk, trot, canter, and jump. The crowd cheered as they watched. Avril could hardly believe that her dream of riding in a competition had finally come true!

When the competition was over, Avril and Mr. Blaze won third place. It was not the first place win she hoped for, but Avril was proud of herself and her horse. She had overcome her fear, risen to the challenge, and gained new confidence as a rider.

Susan, Avril's parents, and the other riding students hugged and congratulated her. They were proud of Avril's win, and they were proud of her for getting past her fears and helping her horse stay calm.

Avril and Mr. Blaze had helped each other overcome their anxiety, and because of that, they had started to develop a bond of friendship and trust.

Chapter Six

Avril the Role Model

Now that the riding competition was over, Avril and the other students at the riding school had settled back into their normal routine. They went over the basics with their horses, then spent some time working on new skills.

After their riding lessons, Avril and Lucy rode together around the field until their parents came to pick them up.

"I wonder what our next challenge will be," Avril said. "I'm pretty sure we won't have any more competitions for a while."

"You always do love a challenge!" Lucy said, laughing.

"That's right! I have a very long list of riding skills I want to learn."

When they came back to the stable, Susan waved them over and said, "Girls, I have some news for you. The riding school will be hosting Open Week in a few days. That means children who love horses and are interested in riding will come and visit us."

"What age will they be?" Avril asked.

"The first groups to visit will be preschool students," Susan said. "They are too young to start riding lessons, but it's never too early to let them visit and see how much fun it will be!"

"What can we do to help?" Avril asked.

"Your part will be to show the children how much fun it is to ride horses. Avril, since you won a prize in the riding competition, you will be the star of the show!"

The thought of getting to show off her riding skills made Avril very happy.

On the first day of Open Week, a group of preschoolers and their parents arrived. The children were very excited about seeing the horses.

Soon, it was time for the students to show off their riding skills. Avril mounted Mr. Blaze and galloped swiftly around the field. The children's eyes sparkled with excitement, and their cheers filled the air.

As she rode, Avril sat tall in the saddle. She knew the preschool children saw her as a hero.

Once Avril's ride was over, she took Mr. Blaze to his stall in the stable. Then she led Jingle Jangle and a few other gentle horses out for the children to visit.

The preschoolers ran over to talk to her.

"Looks like you have some fans," Susan said.

"I've never had fans before," Avril said, laughing. She looked a bit embarrassed by all the attention they were giving her.

"Well, you do now!" Susan replied. "You are their role model."

The idea of being a role model felt strange to Avril. Not so long ago, Susan and her friend Nancy were her role models. How did things change so fast? Avril wasn't sure she was ready for this new responsibility, but she was determined to do her best.

The preschoolers followed Avril all over Susan's farm. As they did, they asked her endless questions about the horses.

"How did the horses get their names?"

"Do horses like candy?"

"Why do horses flip their tail?"

"Do horses sleep standing up?"

Avril tried to answer each child, but their questions kept coming faster than she could answer them. For every question Avril answered, the children asked half a dozen more, and she didn't know the answer to some of their questions.

Avril also had to make sure the children were safe around the horses. Two preschool teachers came with the group, but Avril still felt responsible for the children's safety.

She said, "Try to keep your voice down. Horses are afraid of loud noises. Also, when you go up to a horse, always talk softly and let it smell your hand."

But the preschool children did not follow Avril's instructions. They shrieked happily and chased each other in the grassy area.

Avril quickly realized that she had no experience dealing with preschool children. *Susan must know how to deal with this*, she thought.

Then she saw Susan talking to the parents on the far side of the field. "Great!" Avril sighed. She knew that for the moment, she was on her own.

All afternoon, the preschoolers followed Avril around like baby ducklings. When it was time for them to go home, Avril breathed a sigh of relief.

During Open Week, Avril went to Susan's farm for a few hours every day. Every time Avril rode Mr. Blaze, she became a role model for a new group of children.

Even as her anxiety grew, Avril was determined to stay in control. "I will answer every question and keep the children safe," she promised herself. But the harder she tried, the more stressed and exhausted she felt.

As the week went on, Avril knew she needed a break. Susan was always around, but sometimes she was busy talking to the preschool teachers or the parents who sometimes came. When she felt overly stressed, she tried to get away from the children for a while and collect her thoughts.

Lucy and some other riding students came over to help with the children, but no matter what they said, the children asked, "Where's Avril? We want to see her!"

Then they started to separate from their groups to look for her.

When the children saw Avril come out of the barn, they were happy again.

One day, one of the little boys took a bucket of horse oats to the stable. Before Avril could stop him, he banged on the door and yelled, "Hey, horse, here's your lunch!"

The loud noise spooked the horse. It tossed its head, backed up suddenly, and kicked the side of the stall. The little boy dropped the bucket, screamed, and ran away.

Avril's heart sank with guilt.

Susan heard the screaming and ran over to find out what happened.

"It's all my fault!" Avril said, sniffing. "I wasn't paying enough attention, and now that little boy will probably be afraid of horses for his entire life!"

Susan walked Avril away from the children and said, "I know you did your best. If it was anyone's fault, it was mine. I should have been closer or asked more students to be here and help you when we have so many children."

"That little boy was imitating me," Avril cried. "He saw me feed the horses, and he wanted to feed them too. I did tell the children to be quiet whenever they are around the horses, but I must not have said it enough, or this wouldn't have happened!"

Avril sobbed loudly. "I don't know why anyone would want me as a role model."

Susan smiled and said, "Avril, it wasn't your fault that the little boy tried to feed the horses. Children naturally try to copy what they see. It is how they learn. That little boy just forgot you asked him to be quiet around the horses. Your kind and respectful treatment of the children and the horses makes you a great role model."

"Thank you, Susan." Avril wiped away her tears. "Learning how to be a role model is a pretty big challenge, especially since I don't have experience with small children. But with your help, I think I can do it!"

"It's great to hear you say that," Susan said. "You are a very determined girl, and you can do anything you put your mind to. Let me know how I can help you, and I'll do whatever I can to help you succeed."

"Let me think about it over the weekend," Avril said, "and I'll let you know what I come up with."

That weekend, Avril found a channel about horseback

riding on YouTube and watched all the beginner videos. Then she made a list of everything people new to horses needed to know.

Using that list, Avril worked with Susan to start a class about horses for young children. In these classes, children would learn how to approach a horse quietly, what it is like to live on a horse farm, and the basics of horse care.

The classes were a big success. Avril watched the children's eyes light up as she talked to them about horses. She watched them learn to speak softly to the horses and gently brush them. She saw their love and respect for the horses growing with each class.

Best of all, the little boy who had tried to feed the horses came back. Avril patiently showed him how to feed the horses without frightening them.

Avril learned that being a good role model was not about being perfect or knowing all the answers. It was about doing your best and being kind and patient.

From then on, Avril happily stepped into the idea of being a role model for the children who visited Susan's farm. Being a role model wasn't always easy, but it was always worthwhile.

Chapter Seven

Avril's Balancing Act

On a warm spring morning, Avril stood at the school bus stop. As she waited, she thought about the horses at Susan's farm.

So much had happened this spring. Avril had learned to ride an energetic new horse, won a ribbon in her first horse show, and become a mentor for young children. Even though she had made mistakes now and then, Avril felt proud of her accomplishments.

Before Avril knew it, the bus had pulled up at the school. As she got out, Avril saw Lucy standing by the school door.

"How are things going at riding school?" Lucy asked. "Sorry I couldn't be there last week, but I had a stomach bug. When you have a sick stomach, riding horses is pretty much out of the question."

"Things are going great!" Avril replied. "Glad you're feeling better. I've been working on a new riding skill. I'll show it to you next time we're there."

"I'm looking forward to seeing it," Lucy said. "But now, I'm worried that I didn't study enough for the science test. I hear there are going to be some pretty tough questions."

"You'll do fine," Avril reassured her. "You always get good grades in science."

Their teacher Mrs. Dutton took attendance. Then she passed out papers for the science test.

Avril was also worried about the test. She knew that she had done her best and studied for the past two days. She'd studied late into the night until she could no longer stay awake. With her other homework, the riding school, and her chores at home, it was impossible to give studying for the test any more time.

Avril read over all the questions before she started answering them. She felt relieved, realizing she knew the answer to every question.

Mrs. Dutton walked between the desks as the students wrote down their answers. "I hope you all took time to study," she said. "This test will count for a large part of your grade."

When the recess bell rang, Avril turned in her test, feeling confident that she did well.

Avril walked out into the school yard and stretched. She thought about Mr. Blaze and all the fun she would have riding him on Saturday.

Then she heard a voice. "Hi, Avril, how do you think you did on the test?" It was Lucy.

"Pretty well, I think."

"I think I did all right, too, but now the geography test we have on Monday has me worried."

"The geography test?" Avril gasped. "What geography test?"

"The one Mrs. Dutton told us about last week. Haven't you been studying for it?"

"No. But I will be!" Avril said, gripped by a sudden wave of panic. She had completely forgotten about it!

When Avril got home from school, she said, "Mom, I have a geography test on Monday, so I won't be able to go to the riding school on Saturday as I planned.

It would take too much time away from studying."

"I am glad you are being more serious about your schoolwork," her mother answered, "I'll let Susan know so she won't expect you."

"Thanks!" Avril said as she grabbed a snack and headed to her room to study.

On Saturday morning, Avril headed straight to the library a few streets away. She found books and looked at maps about every possible topic on the test. As she did her best to focus, she couldn't help but think about her friends at the riding school and all the fun they were having. It was a beautiful sunny day, but she was stuck inside studying. Over and over, Avril had to bring her mind back to the task at hand.

When the library was ready to close, Avril checked out several books and took them home. All evening and on Sunday, Avril studied every minute she could.

For Avril, Monday came all too soon. "Did you get enough sleep?" her mother asked. "I saw your light on late last night and knew you were studying."

"I think so," Avril said. "I still can't believe I forgot about that geography test! I wouldn't have studied for it if Lucy hadn't reminded me, and that would have been a disaster."

"We all make mistakes," Avril's father gently reminded her. "With all your studying, I'm sure you'll do well. Remember to think positively!"

"Thanks," Avril said as she got up from the breakfast table. "I hope you're right!"

As Avril rode the bus to school, she repeatedly told herself, "I am a good student, and I can do this!"

But when Mrs. Dutton handed out the geography tests, Avril's confidence started to waver.

Mrs. Dutton could sense that the students were nervous. "Just relax and do your best," she said.

Avril looked over the questions and felt a sinking feeling in her stomach. She thought she knew most of the answers, but she didn't have near the level of confidence she usually felt when taking a test. She glanced at the classroom wall and noticed all the maps had been taken down.

Avril frowned as she looked at the maps on the test. She knew the shape of most of the European countries but was unsure of a few. She did her best to concentrate, taking the questions one at a time. When she turned in the test, she was very worried about her grade.

As Avril rode the bus home from school, the geography test still weighed heavily on her.

When she opened the door, her mother said, "Avril, would you like to go out to the riding school? I know you missed being with the horses over the weekend."

"We thought it would be a fun way for you to unwind," her father added.

"Sure!" Avril said. "I could use some fun after all that studying and test-taking."

On the way to Susan's farm, Avril thought more about the geography test than the horses. She thought about the questions that she had been unsure of and wondered if she got them right.

Avril greeted Susan, and then walked into the stable and mounted Mr. Blaze. Everything she did on her ride around the field felt strangely awkward. Even normal galloping made her feel uneasy. Jumps that used to bring Avril joy now felt like a struggle—it was difficult just to stay balanced on Mr. Blaze's back.

Susan watched quietly with concern in her eyes.

When Avril finished her ride, Susan asked, "Would you like to help me clean the tack and straighten up the stables?"

"Sure!" Avril said. "You know how much I love being around the horses!"

Avril went from stall to stall, brushing the horses. Then she made sure all the riding equipment was hung in its proper place, but a heavy tiredness from her lack of sleep soon took over. As Avril brushed Jingle Jangle, the soothing sound of the gentle horse's breathing almost put her to sleep.

As she was nodding off, Susan stepped into the stable. "Avril," she began, "we have the preschool group coming in a few days for a stable tour. Could you help?"

"Sure!" Avril said, trying to sound more awake than she was. "It's always fun to help the little kids learn about horses."

After Susan left, Avril took a deep breath and sat down in the hay. The commitments she already had for the coming week ran through her mind like a speeding train. She had homework, a special project for science

class, a book she needed to read for a book report, and chores around the house. Avril started to feel completely overwhelmed.

"No matter what, I won't let Susan down," Avril promised herself. "I will make sure everything at the riding school is perfect for the stable tour!"

When her parents came to pick her up, Avril told them about the stable tour and how excited she was to help.

"Are you sure you'll have time for that?" her mother asked. "Remember, your grandparents will be visiting, and we have some family activities planned. You also have homework."

"I'll manage," Avril said.

On the day of the stable tour, Avril arrived early and went to work. She was tired and stressed but felt proud of all she had accomplished.

But as she was setting up the last stable, Avril gasped in horror. She remembered she had promised to help organize Lucy's birthday party. Lucy's birthday was only a few days away, and she hadn't planned a thing!

Avril wanted to get away from everyone. She was too overwhelmed to deal with the preschoolers, Susan, or anyone else. Panicked, she ran into the barn to hide. She curled up in a corner and soon fell into a deep sleep.

When Avril woke up, her mother and father were looking at her. "Are you alright?" her mother asked. "We've been looking for you everywhere."

Tears welled up in Avril's eyes. "No, I'm not," she cried. "I thought I could do it all. But instead, I've let everyone down." She sobbed even louder.

Avril's mother hugged her and whispered, "I know you don't want to let anyone down. You tried your best, but it was just too much."

"But I should have been able to do it!" Avril wailed.

Avril's father smiled. "Don't be so hard on yourself," he said. "It's okay to feel this way, and it's okay to ask for help. We're here for you."

"That's right," her mother added. "You don't have to say yes to everything someone asks you to do, and you don't have to juggle everything on your own."

When they got home, Avril and her parents went over her schedule. Avril did her best to remember all her commitments and listed them on a tablet.

Avril's parents bought her a planner to keep in her notebook. She used it to write down her homework assignments and tests. She also wrote down the days and times of her riding lessons and things she promised to do at home. This helped her keep track of what she needed and wanted to do.

The next day, Avril's mother called Susan to explain the situation. She said, "Avril has a very full schedule for the next few weeks. She might not have time to do extra projects at the stables until school is out for the summer."

"Thanks for letting me know," Susan said. "In the future, I will remind Avril that it's fine to say no if she has too many other things to do."

With the help of Susan and her parents, Avril organized a small birthday party for Lucy and her friends at the riding school. The party was a success, and everyone had a fun time.

Avril realized that life can sometimes feel like a non-stop juggling act. Sometimes it's hard to know how many balls you can juggle, and no matter how hard you try, balls will sometimes get dropped. But with the help of her parents and friends, Avril felt confident that she could always figure out a way to make it all work.

Chapter Eight

A Season of Change

The alarm clock in Avril's bedroom was going off at full volume.

She tried to open her eyes, squinting at the bright beam of sunlight that was coming through the window.

Then she realized what day it was. The day she'd been dreading had finally arrived. This was the last day Mrs. Dutton would be her teacher.

"Are you coming down to breakfast?" her mother called.

"In a minute," Avril answered, trying to wake up enough to get her feet into her slippers.

"You don't want to be late for your teacher's last day," her mom said, "or miss the party your class is having for her."

"I know," Avril said as she made her way down the stairs. "I just wish she wasn't leaving."

Avril liked having Mrs. Dutton as a teacher. Not only that, but she was used to how Mrs. Dutton did things. She liked things the way they were and didn't want them to change. But last week, Mrs. Dutton told the class that her husband had been offered a promotion, and they had to move right away. She also told the class that she had been offered a position at a school that focused on teaching about the environment, and she would be starting there in the fall.

"Change is part of life," her father said as he picked up the pieces of the birdhouse they had been making the night before and sat down at the breakfast table. "Things can't always stay the same. There are just a few more weeks of school before summer vacation, so even if Mrs. Dutton weren't leaving, you wouldn't have her as a teacher much longer."

"I know," Avril said sadly.

Avril never liked it when her parents said things like that. Of course, she knew she would have a new teacher in the fall. That was a change she would have to accept, but she didn't want to deal with the stress of changing teachers now.

During her bus ride to school, Avril thought about what she would say to Mrs. Dutton. She didn't want to make her feel bad about leaving, but at the same time, she wanted to let her know how much she would miss her.

When Avril got to school, the classroom was decorated with colorful balloons and streamers. She also saw a large cake and paper plates on a fold-up table. Mrs. Dutton stood in front of the classroom, talking to the principal.

A poster that said, "Goodbye, Mrs. Dutton!" was on the table near the cake. Students were standing in line to sign it. Soon, it was Avril's turn. She hadn't thought of anything that felt special enough to say, but she had to write something. She picked up a red marker, signed her name, and wrote, "Good luck at your new school! I'll miss you!"

Then Avril got a piece of cake and sat down at her desk. As she ate it, she thought of all the good times she'd had in Mrs. Dutton's class. Avril tried her best not to cry, but she couldn't stop a few tears from flowing down her cheeks.

"Can I have your attention, please?" Mrs. Dutton said, trying to hold her tears back.

The chatter in the classroom stopped, and the students who were still standing went to their seats.

"First of all, thank you for the wonderful party," she said, smiling. "I will always remember you, and what a joy it was being your teacher."

All the students clapped. Then Mrs. Dutton held up her hand to quiet the room.

"Someone is here who I want you all to meet," Mrs. Dutton said. "Her name is Miss Adler, and she will be your teacher for the rest of the year."

As she said that, Miss Adler stepped through the door into the classroom.

"Please make her feel welcome," Mrs. Dutton said. The class started to clap again.

Avril clapped along with the other students and did her best to smile, but she wasn't ready to meet this new teacher. She didn't expect someone to replace Mrs. Dutton on the same day she was leaving. She thought this wouldn't happen until tomorrow.

"Hello, everyone," Miss Adler began. "I'm excited to get to know you and be a part of your learning journey."

Again, the students clapped.

"Does anyone have any questions?" Miss Adler asked.

A boy raised his hand. "Do we have to sit in the same seats?"

Miss Adler looked towards the principal, and he nodded. "Since you have a new teacher, I see nothing wrong with you having a new seat. You can all change seats if you want," he said.

A buzz of excitement filled the room. Nearly all the students jumped up, pulled the books out of their desks, and selected a new seat.

Avril was dismayed to see her friend Lucy get up and move to a seat near the window.

"Avril, do you want to sit next to me over here?" Lucy asked.

"Thanks, but I think I'll stay where I am," Avril answered. She wanted to sit by Lucy, but staying in her regular seat made her feel secure.

As the day went on, Avril realized that almost everything Miss Adler did was different. The seating change was just the beginning. Miss Adler had different ways of teaching, asking questions, and even picking up the papers at the end of the day.

Mrs. Dutton looked on from her desk. Avril hoped that she would tell Miss Adler how things should be done in a classroom, but she kept silent, only occasionally looking up from the papers she was sorting. This made Avril feel even more frustrated.

When the school bell rang, Avril had never been happier to get out of the classroom. When she got home, her parents asked her all sorts of questions about the party and the new teacher. Avril answered them and tried to sound happy. When the questions finally ended, she headed to her room and got lost in a book.

As the week went on, it seemed that hardly anything in Avril's life stayed the same. On Tuesday, her riding lesson was delayed. On Wednesday night, her parents decided to go to the movies without her. This was something they hadn't done in a very long time. They called it a date night, but to Avril, it felt like she was being left out.

On Thursday, Avril looked forward to her riding lesson all day. Finally, something in her life would feel normal again! She could hardly wait to see Susan and tell her about the new teacher and the riding videos she had been watching. She also looked forward to riding Mr. Blaze.

But when Avril got to the riding school, Susan's friend Nancy met her at the gate. "Hi, Avril!" Nancy said. "Susan had to be away today. She asked me to take charge of the riding lessons."

Avril's heart sank. She liked Nancy and enjoyed training with her, but Nancy wasn't Susan. All these changes made Avril feel like she was losing control. It felt like her entire world was collapsing, and she could do nothing to stop it.

The following morning, rain was pouring down. Avril's dad offered to drive her to school so she wouldn't get wet waiting for the bus.

When they were a few streets away from home, he said, "Looks like there's some road work ahead. We'll have to take another route."

Avril sighed. She did not want to take a different route to school. Her father noticed that she was tense and said, "Don't worry. I'll have you there before the first bell rings."

School was another day of everything being different. Mrs. Dutton was gone now, and Miss Adler was in complete control of the class. She passed out strips of paper for the students to write their names on and put on their desks. "This will help me get to know you," she said.

Avril wondered how much they could really get to know each other before summer vacation.

That afternoon at riding school, Avril was happy that Susan was back. "Hi, Avril! Today, I want you to try riding Blue Bell," Susan said.

"Why can't I ride Mr. Blaze?" Avril asked, looking puzzled.

"This morning, I noticed that Mr. Blaze has a sore spot on his hoof," Susan said. "I think we should let him rest until the vet has a chance to look at it."

Avril was getting stressed.

"I'm sure you and Blue Bell will get along great," Susan said. "Blue Bell isn't quite as spirited as Mr. Blaze, but she's a more active horse than Jingle Jangle."

Avril felt tears flowing out of her eyes. Tears she couldn't stop. "Why does EVERYTHING have to keep changing?" she moaned loudly. "Every time I feel like things are under control, they change! I have to get used to a new teacher, my parents go to the movies without me, my father had to take a detour to get me to school, and now THIS!"

Avril wanted to run and hide in the barn, but it was too late. Everyone at the riding school, including her friend Lucy, had heard her outburst and saw her crying. She was angry and embarrassed at the same time.

Susan hugged Avril. "You know, Avril, not all changes are bad," Susan said.

Avril kept on crying, wishing she could disappear.

"Think about the seasons," Susan continued. "In the winter, everything is frozen. But after a few months, spring comes. Then the flowers will bloom again, and caterpillars become butterflies."

Lucy chimed in, "Remember how nervous you were when you first met Mr. Blaze? You didn't want to ride him at all. Now you are as bonded to him as to Jingle Jangle."

After crying, Avril felt better and went to the bathroom to wash her face. When she came out, she decided to ride Blue Bell. It wasn't her best ride ever, but she still enjoyed it.

When she went home that night, Avril thought about what Susan and Lucy said. Sometimes change can be good. She took out her notebook and made a list of the changes she would try to accept.

The next day at school, Avril decided to talk to Miss Adler after class. To her surprise, she found that they shared a love for reading. Within a few minutes, the conversation moved from books to horses. Avril found out that Miss Adler's grandfather had a horse farm, and she grew up riding. Avril felt her resistance to having Miss Adler as a teacher start to crumble.

At her next riding lesson, Avril learned that Susan had bought a new horse named Starlight. When Susan told her about Starlight, she immediately asked to ride her.

One evening, Avril's mother said, "Avril, we are proud of all you have accomplished in the past year. Moving to a new place is not easy, but you have managed to not only make new friends but gain new interests as well."

"And you have a more positive attitude," her father added. "When you learn to accept changes, life can be a lot more fun!"

Avril smiled at her parents. "Things are always going to change," she said, "but now I know that changes really can bring good things."

Each book that we have published has a free audio version available. To download the audiobook for *Horses, My Beginnings,* **all you have to do is scan the QR code** or visit: www.littlebigpage.com/horses

If you have any problems or questions, feel free to contact us at help@littlebigpage.com

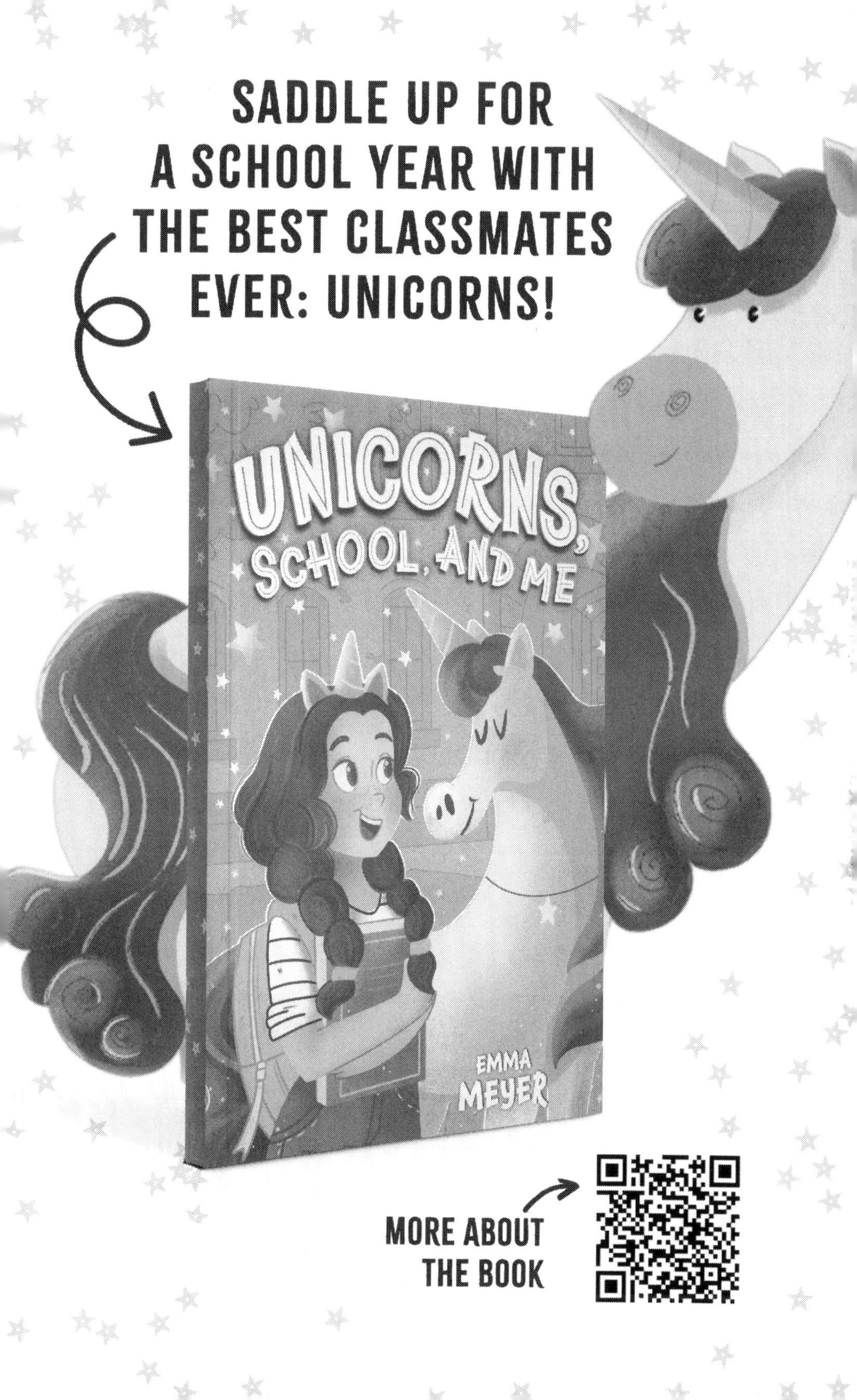
SADDLE UP FOR
A SCHOOL YEAR WITH
THE BEST CLASSMATES
EVER: UNICORNS!
UNICORNS, SCHOOL, AND ME
EMMA
MEYER
MORE ABOUT
THE BOOK

Made in the USA
Columbia, SC
12 April 2025